Keto Fat Bombs beginners

A guide to simple yet delicious & healthy weight loss plans for busy people

-- By Linda Underwood --

Copyright © 2019 by Linda Underwood

All rights reserved. No part of this guide may be reproduced in any form without permission in writing from the publisher, except for brief quotations used for publishable articles or reviews.

Legal Disclaimer

The information contained in this book and its contents is not designed to replace any form of medical or professional advice; and is not meant to replace the need for independent medical, financial, legal, or other professional advice or services that may be required. The content and information in this book have been provided for educational and entertainment purposes only.

The content and information contained in this book have been compiled from sources deemed reliable, and they are accurate to the best of the Author's knowledge, information, and belief. However, the Author cannot guarantee its accuracy and validity and therefore cannot be held liable for any errors and/or omissions. Further, changes are periodically made to this book as needed. Where appropriate and/or necessary, you must consult a professional (including but not limited to your doctor, attorney, financial advisor, or other such professional) before using any of the suggested remedies, techniques, and/or information in this book.

Upon using this book's contents and information, you agree to hold harmless the Author from any damages, costs, and expenses, including any legal fees potentially resulting from the application of any of the information in this book. This disclaimer applies to any loss, damages, or injury caused by the use and application of this book's contents, whether directly or indirectly, whether for breach of contract, tort, negligence, personal injury, criminal intent, or under any other circumstance.

You agree to accept all risks of using the information presented in this book.

You agree that by continuing to read this book, where appropriate and/or necessary, you shall consult a professional (including but not limited to your doctor, attorney, financial advisor, or other such professional) before using any of the suggested remedies, techniques, or information in this book.

TABLE OF CONTENTS

INTRODUCTION 6
Chapter 1 The Ketogenic Diet and Fat Bombs 8
Chapter 2 Sweet Fat Bombs 11
    1. Almond Butter-Chocolate Bombs 11
    2. Chocolate Fat Bombs 13
    3. Peanut Butter Bites 15
    4. Sweet Cream Truffles 17
    5. Raspberry and Peanut Butter Truffles 19
    6. Almond Joy Balls 21
    7. Black and White Peppermint Cups 23
    8. Chocolate Peanut Butter Chocolate Cups 25
    9. Vanilla Mocha Pops 27
    10. Chocolate Coconut Candies 29
    11. Cinnamon Coconut Balls 31
    12. Avocado Chocolate Pudding Pops 33
    13. White Chocolate Fat Bombs 35
    14. Velvet Bombs 37
    15. Espresso Fat Bombs 39
    16. Peanut Butter Chocolate Chip Bombs 41
    17. Pumpkin Spice Bombs 43
    18. Berries and Cream Fat Bombs 45
    20. Almond Butter Fat Bombs 49
    21. Fudge Fat Bombs 51
    22. Almond Fat Bombs 53
    23. Coconut Almond Fat Bombs 55
    24. Chocolate Macadamia Fat Bombs 57
    25. Valentine's Day Fat Bombs 59
    26. Spiced Cocoa Coolers 61
    27. Walnut Chocolate and Orange Fat Bombs 63
    28. Coconut Chocolate Candies 65
    29. Coconut Fat Bombs 67

Chapter 3 Savory Fat Bombs... 69
    1. Cheesy Jalapeno Fat Bombs 69
    2. Avocado and Egg Fat Bombs 71
    3. Salmon Bites 73
    4. Salmon Fat Bombs 75
    5. Bacon and Egg Fat Bombs...77
    6. Bacon and Guacamole Fat Bombs 79
    7. Mediterranean Fat Bombs..81
    8. Pizza Fat Bombs 83
    9. Cheesy Pesto Fat Bombs 85
    10. Herbed Cheese Fat Bombs 87
    11. Pork Belly Fat Bombs.. 89
    12. Stilton and Chive Fat Bombs...91
    13. Bacon Ranch Fat Bombs 93
    14. Crispy Savory Bacon Fat Bombs 95
    15. Jalapeno Pepper Fat Bombs 97
    16. Waldorf Salad Fat Bombs 99
    17. Brie and Pecan Prosciutto Fat Bombs 101
    18. Zucchini Fat Bombs 103
    19. Sardine Fat Bombs 105
    20. Smoked mackerel Fat Bombs 107
    21. Anchovy Fat Bombs 109
    22. Bacon Fat Bombs..111
    23. Buttered Bacon Fat Bombs 113
    24. Sesame Fat Bombs 115
    25. Cheese Meatballs 117
    26. Scotch Eggs 119
    27. Sausage Balls 121

28. Mozzarella Fat Bombs..*123*

29. Cheesy Fat Bombs *125*

30. Spinach Fat Bombs *127*

CONCLUSION *129*

INTRODUCTION

If you are following a low-carb, high-fat Ketogenic diet, then keto fat bombs are about to be your new favorite snack. Fat bombs are like energy balls, but instead of sugar and carbs, they are made with mostly healthy fats, which make them handy for a quick breakfast, pre-or post-workout meal or an afternoon snack. These sweet and savory fat bombs are perfect for fat fasts and help you boost your fat intake. These delicious, high-fat snacks are ideal for a high-fat, low-carb Ketogenic diet, and also a great alternative to sugary, carb-filled treats. Your keto diet doesn't have to be boring.

You can enjoy your diet while you lose weight. This book is a collection of the most delicious sweet and savory fat bombs, with seasonal ingredients so you can avoid boredom and lose weight all the year-round. These healthy high fat keto bombs are perfect for on-the-go energy, curing between meals hunger and a perfect treat to fill your sweet tooth cravings. This keto fat bombs cookbook includes simple to prep and easy to make delicious fat bomb recipes that subdue your cravings and gives you a boost of energy.

These sweet and savory fat bombs will fill you up in between meals, give you an energy boost and help shed those stubborn pounds. These simple recipes include easy-to-find ingredients, so you will always have something satisfying and scrumptious to snack on. Make these keto bombs part of your low carb diet to easily increase your energy, satisfy your sugar cravings, and even impress your non-keto friends. This book offers dozens of tasty fat bomb recipes, which will help keep your macros in balance, prevent cravings for non-diet foods and trigger weight loss.

Chapter 1 The Ketogenic Diet and Fat Bombs

In the 1920s, researchers discovered that a low-carb, high-fat keto style diet is needed to treat epilepsy in children. This treatment was used widely. However, with the invent of modern epilepsy medicine, the popularity of the keto diet begin to fade. In the early 1990s, keto diet made a comeback. During that time, a TV show revealed that a low-carb, moderate protein and high-fat diet could trigger weight loss. The diets become hugely popular and currently, it is the most popular weight loss diet.

Health benefits of the Ketogenic diet

1. Weight loss: It is scientifically proven that this diet can help dieters lose weight.
2. Appetite control: The diet is a high-fat diet. Fat has an effect on dieters and they eat less naturally because they feel less hungry.
3. Increase good cholesterol levels: The keto diet increases your good cholesterol levels and lowers bad cholesterol levels.
4. Increases energy levels: Eating carb-rich foods produce glycogen and makes you tired and lethargic. With keto, your body is in ketosis and full of energy.
5. Reverse type 2 diabetes: Diabetes has become a global health problem. Eating a keto style diet can help you prevent diabetes symptoms.

Fat bombs

Fat bombs are simply high fat and low carb snacks that you can use as a quick breakfast, as a quick mid-afternoon snack, as a pre- or after- workout snack, or as extra fuel during your day.

Keto fat bomb facts

1. Fat bombs contain useful and healthy fats: Most Ketogenic fat bombs contain mainly coconut oil, butter, coconut or almond butter as the main ingredient. All these ingredients are healthy.
2. They are smaller: Because of high-fat contents, the fat bomb cannot be eaten in big portions. This is the reason the fat bombs have the size of small balls or mini-muffins.
3. They can be sweet or savory: Fat bombs can be divided into two groups: sweet and savory. The sweet fat bombs are made with keto-approved sweeteners and savory fat bombs include ingredients like bacon, jalapeno, eggs, meat products, and spices.
4. They may contain seeds and nuts. Sometimes they contain nuts and seeds but not in excess because nuts are high in carb.
5. Storing: Refrigeration is the best-recommended storage for fat bombs.

Best ways to consume fat bombs

1. You can eat them as pre or post-workout snacks instead of carb-rich snacks.
2. They can be used as a quick hit of energy, especially when you don't have time to cook keto meals.
3. Always add fat bombs in your keto meals once in a while. They will help you meet your Ketogenic lifestyle target easily and also provide you with enough fat you need for your daily activity.
4. You can use keto fat bombs to celebrate special seasons and occasions like wedding, birthday party, Christmas, Valentine's day, etc.

Some common ingredients in fat bomb recipes

1. Useful facts: Including coconut butter, almond butter, cocoa butter, coconut oil, coconut milk, coconut cream, butter, ghee, bacon fat, and avocado oil.
2. Flavors: Like vanilla extract, dark chocolate, cocoa powder, salt, peppermint extract, spices.

3. Textures: Like cocoa nibs, almonds, pecans, walnuts, chia seeds, bacon bits, shredded coconut, etc.

General fat bomb preparation steps:

1. First step: Combine all the needed ingredients in a bowl, a food processor or a blender. If you are using solid fat, melt it slightly in the microwave.
2. Second step: Make small balls. To make small balls, pour the mixture into muffin cups or into a baking pan or just use your hands to form the needed shape.
3. Third step: Refrigerate them for several hours for the mixtures to become solid. You can cut them into smaller sizes if using a baking pan.

Appliances you may need

- Oven
- Microwave
- Skillet
- Saucepan
- Refrigerator
- Boiler
- Hand mixer, etc.

Chapter 2 Sweet Fat Bombs

1. Almond Butter-Chocolate Bombs

| Prep time: 10 minutes | Cook time: 5 minutes | Servings: 12 |

Ingredients

- Solid coconut oil – ½ cup
- No-sugar added almond butter – ¼ cup
- Sugar-free chocolate chips

Method

1. Line a mini-muffin pan with paper liners.
2. In a bowl, combine almond butter, coconut oil, and chocolate chips.
3. Microwave on high for 1 minute. Stir and microwave in 1-minute increments. Stirring after each, until the ingredients well blended.
4. Divide the mixture evenly among the prepared muffin cups.
5. Freeze until firm, about 2 hours.

Nutritional Facts Per Serving

- Calories: 137
- Fat: 13g
- Carb: 1g
- Protein: 1g

2. *Chocolate Fat Bombs*

| Prep time: 15 minutes | Cook time: 5 minutes | Servings: 6 |

Ingredients

- Keto cooking spray
- Sugar-free chocolate chips – ½ cup
- Unsalted butter – 1 Tbsp.
- Heavy cream – ¼ cup

Method

1. Spray a 12-cavity truffle mold with cooking spray. Set aside.
2. Combine the butter, cream, and chocolate chips.
3. Microwave on high for 30 seconds. Stir well. Microwave in 10-second increments until the ingredients are well blended. Do not overcook.
4. Pour the mixture into truffle molds and freeze for 30 minutes.
5. Unmold the truffles onto a plate and chill until set, about 1 hour.
6. Serve.

Nutritional Facts Per Serving

- Calories: 184
- Fat: 16g
- Carb: 2g
- Protein: 1g

3. Peanut Butter Bites

| Prep time: 15 minutes | Cook time: 5 minutes | Servings: 12 |

Ingredients

- Creamy no-sugar-added peanut butter – ½ cup
- Unsalted butter – 8 Tbsp.
- Swerve confectioners' sweetener – 2 Tbsp.
- Vanilla extract – 1 tsp.

Method

1. In a bowl, combine the butter, peanut butter, and sweetener.
2. Microwave on high in 30- second increments, stirring after each until the mixture is completely melted.
3. Add the vanilla and stir until all the sweetener is dissolved.
4. Pour the mixture into a 24-cavity truffle mold.

5. Freeze for 2 to 4 hours, until set. Unmold the bites.
6. Set in the freezer and serve.

Nutritional Facts Per Serving

- Calories: 136
- Fat: 13g
- Carb: 1g
- Protein: 3g

4. Sweet Cream Truffles

| Prep time: 30 minutes | Cook time: 5 minutes | Servings: 6 |

Ingredients

- Heavy cream – 2 cups
- Swerve confectioners sweetener – ½ cup
- Sugar-free chocolate chips – ½ cup
- Unsalted butter – 1 Tbsp.

Method

1. Line a rimmed baking sheet with parchment paper. Set aside.
2. Combine the cream and sweetener in a saucepan.
3. Cook over medium heat, stirring frequently until the mixture turns light brown and thickens slightly about 5 to 6 minutes.
4. Transfer the mixture to a bowl and chill until firm, about 1 hour.
5. When the mixture is firm, form it into 12 small balls.
6. Arrange the balls on a plate and chill in the refrigerator while you prepare the coating.

7. In a bowl, combine the chocolate chips and butter. Microwave on high for 30 seconds, stir.
8. Let stand for 1 minute and stir again to melt any remaining un-melted chocolate or butter.
9. Spear each sweet cream ball with a fork and dip into the chocolate coating.
10. Place each coated truffle on the prepared pan.
11. Chill in the refrigerator for 2 hours and serve.

Nutritional Facts Per Serving

- Calories: 382
- Fat: 37g
- Carb: 4g
- Protein: 3g

5. Raspberry and Peanut Butter Truffles

| Prep time: 5 minutes | Cook time: 15 minutes | Servings: 10 |

Ingredients

- Raspberries – 1 cup, chopped
- No sugar added peanut butter – 1 cup
- Whipped cream – 1 cup

Method

1. Preheat oven at 355F.
2. In a blender, add raspberries, peanut butter, whipped cream and blend until smooth.
3. Transfer into cupcake molds and bake for 15 minutes.
4. Serve.

Nutritional Facts Per Serving

- Calories: 193
- Fat: 16.8g
- Carb: 6.9g
- Protein: 6.9g

6. *Almond Joy Balls*

| Prep time: 15 minutes | Cook time: 0 minutes | Servings: 4 |

Ingredients

- Almond butter – 2 Tbsp.
- Coconut oil – 2 Tbsp. melted
- Cocoa powder – 2 Tbsp.
- Coconut flour – 1 Tbsp.
- Splenda to taste

Method

1. Mix the coconut oil and the cocoa powder.
2. Add the almond butter and mix until smooth.
3. Add the coconut flour and sweetener.
4. Form into balls.

5. Place the mixture on wax paper.
6. Freeze and serve.

Nutritional Facts Per Serving

- Calories: 128
- Fat: 12.8g
- Carb: 3.7g
- Protein: 2.3g

7. Black and White Peppermint Cups

| Prep time: 5 minutes | Cook time: 0 minutes | Servings: 2 |

Ingredients for the peppermint layer

- Coconut butter – ¾ cup
- Coconut – 1/3, shredded
- Coconut oil – 1 Tbsp.
- Peppermint extract – ½ tsp.

For the cocoa layer

- Coconut oil – 2 Tbsp.
- Cocoa powder – 2 tsp.

Method

1. For the peppermint layer: combine all of the ingredients.
2. Mix well and pour into mini-muffin tins, filling to ½ full.

3. Put in the refrigerator for 15 minutes or until hard.
4. For the cocoa layer: mix the ingredients.
5. Pour the mixture over the hard peppermint layer, filling the cups or molds.
6. Return to the fridge and cool until firm.
7. Serve.

Nutritional Facts Per Serving

- Calories: 442
- Fat: 45.1g
- Carb: 2.3g
- Protein: 2.8g

8. Chocolate Peanut Butter Chocolate Cups

| Prep time: 15 minutes | Cook time: 10 minutes | Servings: 12 |

Ingredients

- Coconut oil – ¾ cup
- Cocoa powder – ¼ cup
- Peanut butter – ¼ cup
- Coconut oil – 1 tsp.
- Liquid stevia – 30 drops

Method

1. Heat ¾ cup coconut oil until melted. Then divide into 3 bowls.
2. In one bowl of oil, stir in the cocoa powder until completely dissolved.
3. Add about 6 drops of liquid stevia. Stir to mix.
4. In another bowl of oil, add the peanut butter. Blend until smooth. Add 6 drops of liquid stevia.
5. In the last bowl, add the 1 tsp. coconut oil. Add the remaining liquid stevia.
6. Divide the chocolate mixture into 12 small cups.
7. Refrigerate for 10 minutes or until firm.

8. When firm, divide the peanut butter mixture over the chocolate mixture.
9. Return to the fridge until set.
10. When firm, divide the coconut oil mixture over the hard peanut butter layer.
11. Chill until firm and serve.

Nutritional Facts Per Serving

- Calories: 153
- Fat: 16.6g
- Carb: 2.1g
- Protein: 1.7g

9. Vanilla Mocha Pops

| Prep time: 15 minutes | Cook time: 10 minutes | Servings: 4 |

Ingredients for the vanilla layer

- Unsalted butter – 4 Tbsp.
- Heavy cream – 2 Tbsp.
- Vanilla extract – ½ tsp.

For the mocha layer

- Coconut oil – 4 Tbsp.
- Cocoa powder – 1 ½ Tbsp.
- Coffee extract – ½ tsp.
- Liquid stevia – ¾ tsp.

Method

1. For the vanilla layer: soften the butter in a microwave until melts.

2. Stir in the heavy cream and vanilla.
3. Pour the mixture into muffin tins, about ½ full.
4. Place in the refrigerator until firm, about 15 minutes.
5. For the mocha layer: mix all the ingredients and pour the mixture over the vanilla layer, filling each cup to the top.

Nutritional Facts Per Serving

- Calories: 502
- Fat: 56.3g
- Carb: 5.3g
- Protein: 1.3g

10. Chocolate Coconut Candies

| Prep time: 20 minutes | Cook time: 0 minutes | Servings: 6 |

Ingredients

- Coconut oil – 1 cup, softened (not melted)
- Vanilla extract – 1 tsp.
- Sugar equivalent – 2 Tbsp.
- Celtic sea salt – ½ tsp.
- Cocoa powder – 4 Tbsp. unsweetened
- Almond butter - 2 Tbsp.

Method

1. In a food processor, mix together all of the ingredients until the mixture is smooth.

2. Scoop tbsp. of the mixture. Drop each tbsp. of the mixture into a parchment or waxed paper with desiccated coconut.
3. Refrigerate the candies until solid.
4. Serve.

Nutritional Facts Per Serving

- Calories: 357
- Fat: 39.8g
- Carb: 3.5g
- Protein: 1.6g

11. Cinnamon Coconut Balls

| Prep time: 90 minutes | Cook time: 5 minutes | Servings: 12 |

Ingredients for the balls

- Coconut or almond butter – 1 cup
- Full-fat coconut milk - 1 cup
- Coconut – 1 cup, shredded, unsweetened
- Stevia powder extract – 1 tsp.
- Vanilla extract – 1 tsp.
- Cinnamon – ½ tsp.
- Nutmeg – ½ tsp.

Method
1. Put a few inches of water into a saucepan.
2. Place a glass bowl over, creating a double boiler.

3. Except for the shredded coconut, put all of the ingredients into the bowl. Heat over medium heat, mixing the ingredients until melted. Mix well.
4. Place the bowl in the fridge, cooling the mixture for about 30 minutes until it is hard enough to roll into balls.
5. Roll into a 1-inch ball and then roll into shredded coconut.
6. Place the balls on a plate and then refrigerate for 1 hour.
7. Serve.

Nutritional Facts Per Serving

- Calories: 142
- Fat: 13.8g
- Carb: 5.3g
- Protein: 1.4g

12. Avocado Chocolate Pudding Pops

| Prep time: 15 minutes | Cook time: 0 minutes | Servings: 10 |

Ingredients

- Unsweetened coconut milk – 6 Tbsp.
- Coconut oil – 2 Tbsp.
- Cocoa powder – 2 Tbsp.
- Avocado – 2 ripe
- Unsweetened chocolate – 2 ounces, chopped
- Stevia extract – ¼ tsp.
- Low-carb powdered sweetener - ¼ cup
- Vanilla extract – ½ tsp.

- Pinch salt

Method

1. Puree the avocado in a blender until smooth.
2. Add the sweetener, cocoa powder, coconut milk, stevia extract, vanilla, and salt. Continue processing on low until well mixed.
3. Melt the coconut oil and chocolate together in a microwave until smooth.
4. Spoon ½ of the mixture into popsicle molds and then tap the molds on a hard flat surface to release air bubbles.
5. Spoon the remaining mixture into the mold. Tap once again.
6. Press wooden Popsicle sticks into the mold, about 2/3 deep.
7. Freeze until set.
8. Serve.

Nutritional Facts Per Serving

- Calories: 197
- Fat: 19.8g
- Carb: 5.4g
- Protein: 2.4g

13. White Chocolate Fat Bombs

| Prep time: 10 minutes | Cook time: 5 minutes | Servings: 2 |

Ingredients

- Cocoa butter – ¼ cup
- Coconut oil – ¼ cup
- Vanilla flavored stevia – 10 drops

Method

1. Melt together cocoa butter and coconut oil over low heat.
2. Add stevia and mix.
3. Fill 8 molds with the mixture.
4. Chill for 1 hour. Remove from molds.
5. Serve.

Nutritional Facts Per Serving

- Calories: 125
- Fat: 10g
- Carb: 0g

- Protein: 0g

14. Velvet Bombs

| Prep time: 10 minutes | Cook time: 5 minutes | Servings: 24 |

Ingredients

- 90% dark chocolate – 3 ½ oz.
- Cream cheese – 4 ½ oz. softened
- Butter – 3 ½ oz. softened
- Stevia – 3 Tbsp.
- Vanilla extract – 1 tsp.
- Red food coloring – 4 drops
- Heavy cream – 1/3 cup, whipped

Method

1. Melt the chocolate in a microwave.
2. Combine the remaining ingredients, except the whipping cream, with a hand mixer.
3. Add the melted chocolate and mix for 2 minutes.
4. Fill a piping bag with the mixture and transfer the fat bomb mixture into a lined tray.
5. Refrigerate for 40 minutes.
6. Top with whipped cream, cut into servings and serve.

Nutritional Facts Per Serving

- Calories: 85
- Fat: 9g
- Carb: 1.2g
- Protein: 1g

15. Espresso Fat Bombs

| Prep time: 10 minutes | Cook time: 4 minutes | Servings: 24 |

Ingredients

- Unsalted butter – 5 Tbsp. softened
- Cream cheese – 3 oz. softened
- Espresso – 2 oz.
- Coconut oil – 4 Tbsp.
- Heavy whipping cream – 2 Tbsp.
- Monk fruit sweetener – 2 Tbsp.

Method

1. Melt together all ingredients except the sweetener in a double boiler for 3 to 4 minutes.
2. Add the sweetener and mix with a hand mixer.
3. Spoon the mixture into silicone muffin molds.

4. Freeze for 4 hours.
5. Remove fat bombs from the molds and serve.

Nutritional Facts Per Serving

- Calories: 63
- Fat: 6.8g
- Carb: 0.3g
- Protein: 0.3g

16. Peanut Butter Chocolate Chip Bombs

| Prep time: 10 minutes | Cook time: 0 minutes | Servings: 24 |

Ingredients

- Cream cheese – 8 oz.
- Peanut butter – 6 to 8 Tbsp.
- Butter – 2 Tbsp.
- Vanilla - 1 Tbsp.
- Xylitol – 2 Tbsp.
- Dark chocolate chips – 9 oz.

Method

1. Mix all the ingredients except the chocolate chips with a hand mixer.
2. Stir in chocolate chips.
3. Place the mixture in silicone candy molds.

4. Freeze for 4 hours.
5. Serve.

Nutritional Facts Per Serving

- Calories: 63
- Fat: 6g
- Carb: 1.2g
- Protein: 1.5g

17. Pumpkin Spice Bombs

Prep time: 10 minutes	Cook time: 10 minutes	Servings: 24

Ingredients

- Pecans – ½ cup
- Coconut oil – ½ cup
- Cream cheese – 4 oz. softened
- Pumpkin puree – ½ cup
- Monk fruit sweetener – ¼ cup
- Pumpkin pie spice – 2 tsp.
- Cinnamon – ¼ tsp.

Method

1. Toast the pecans in a pan until fragrant.
2. Melt cream cheese and coconut oil over medium-low heat until combined.
3. Mix all ingredients in a bowl.
4. Spoon the mixture into the silicone molds, top with toasted pecans, and sprinkle with cinnamon.
5. Freezes for 4 hours.
6. Serve.

Nutritional Facts Per Serving

- Calories: 78
- Fat: 8.2g
- Carb: 1g
- Protein: 0.7g

18. Berries and Cream Fat Bombs

| Prep time: 5 minutes | Cook time: 1 minute | Servings: 24 |

Ingredients

- Frozen mixed berries – 2 cups
- Butter – 6 Tbsp. softened
- Cream cheese – 8 oz. softened
- Monk fruit sweetener – 2 Tbsp.
- Vanilla extract – 1 tsp.

Method

1. Microwave frozen berries until thawed, about 1 minute.
2. Blend all ingredients in a food processor.
3. Spoon mixture into silicone molds and freeze overnight.
4. Pop fat bombs out of molds.
5. Serve.

Nutritional Facts Per Serving

- Calories: 61
- Fat: 5.9g
- Carb: 1.4g
- Protein: 0.8g

19. PBJ Fat Bombs

| Prep time: 5 minutes | Cook time: 1 minute | Servings: 30 |

Ingredients

- Coconut oil – ¼ cup + 1 Tbsp.
- Frozen raspberries – 2 cups
- Peanut butter – ¾ cup
- Coconut flour – ¼ cup
- Powdered stevia – 1/8 tsp.

Method

1. Microwave frozen raspberries for 1 minute, until slightly warmed.
2. Blend all ingredients in a food processor.
3. Spoon mixture into silicone molds and freeze for 1 hour.
4. Remove from freezer, pop fat bombs out of molds.
5. Serve.

Nutritional Facts Per Serving

- Calories: 86
- Fat: 7.6g
- Carb: 2g
- Protein: 2.3g

20. Almond Butter Fat Bombs

| Prep time: 10 minutes | Cook time: 1 minute | Servings: 8 |

Ingredients

- Almond butter – ¼ cup
- Coconut oil – ¼ cup
- Cocoa powder – 2 Tbsp.
- Erythritol – ¼ cup

Method

1. Mix together almond butter and coconut oil.
2. Microwave for 30 to 45 seconds or until heated.
3. Add cocoa powder, and erythritol.
4. Pour into silicone molds.
5. Refrigerate for 30 minutes.
6. Serve.

Nutritional Facts Per Serving

- Calories: 189
- Fat: 19.1g
- Carb: 1.4g
- Protein: 3.2g

21. Fudge Fat Bombs

| Prep time: 10 minutes | Cook time: 5 minutes | Servings: 30 |

Ingredients

- Almond butter - 1 cup
- Coconut oil – 1 cup
- Unsweetened cocoa powder – ½ cup
- Coconut flour – 1/3 cup
- Powdered stevia – ¼ tsp.
- Pink Himalayan salt – 1/16 tsp

Method

1. Combine coconut oil and butter and melt over medium heat.
2. Stir in remaining ingredients. Mix well.
3. Pour mixture into silicone molds and put in the freezer to solidify for 2 hours.
4. Serve.

Nutritional Facts Per Serving

- Calories: 144
- Fat: 13.5g
- Carb: 3.6g
- Protein: 2.4g

22. *Almond Fat Bombs*

| Prep time: 10 minutes | Cook time: 5 minutes | Servings: 4 |

Ingredients

- Almond butter – 4 Tbsp.
- Cream cheese - 1 oz.
- Coconut butter – 4 Tbsp.
- Cocoa powder – 1 Tbsp.
- Sugar-free syrup – 2 Tbsp.
- Dark chocolate – 16g

Method

1. Add all the ingredients other than coconut butter in a dish.

2. Microwave in intervals for 15 seconds, stirring frequently, until chocolate and the cream cheese have melted and all the ingredients have incorporated fully.
3. Add coconut butter, and then mix fully.
4. Spoon the batter into 12 portions in a mini-muffin tray.
5. Pop these into a freezer for about 1 hour.
6. Serve.

Nutritional Facts Per Serving

- Calories: 86
- Fat: 7g
- Carb: 3g
- Protein: 2g

23. Coconut Almond Fat Bombs

| Prep time: 10 minutes | Cook time: 0 minutes | Servings: 24 |

Ingredients

- Melted coconut oil – ¾ cup
- Almond butter – 9 ½ Tbsp.
- Liquid stevia – 60 drops
- Cocoa – 3 Tbsp.
- Melted salted butter - 9 drops

Method

1. Mix everything in a bowl.
2. Fill 24 mini muffin molds with this mixture and freeze for 30 minutes.
3. Serve.

Nutritional Facts Per Serving

- Calories: 145
- Fat: 14.7g
- Carb: 1.7g
- Protein: 1.5g

24. Chocolate Macadamia Fat Bombs

| Prep time: 5 minutes | Cook time: 5 to 10 minutes | Servings: 6 |

Ingredients

- Cocoa butter – 2 oz.
- Unsweetened cocoa powder – 2 Tbsp.
- Swerve – 2 Tbsp.
- Chopped macadamias – 4 oz.
- Heavy cream – ¼ cup

Method

1. Melt the cocoa butter in a bowl over a double boiler.
2. Put cocoa powder, and swerve and mix until melted.
3. Add the macadamias and stir in well.
4. Add cream and mix well.
5. Pour in the molds.
6. Cool and place in the freezer.

7. Serve.

Nutritional Facts Per Serving

- Calories: 267
- Fat: 28g
- Carb: 3g
- Protein: 3g

25. Valentine's Day Fat Bombs

Prep time: 5 minutes	Cook time: 5 minutes	Servings: 4

Ingredients

- Coconut oil – 2 oz.
- Cream cheese – 1 ½ oz.
- Sugar-free vanilla syrup – ½ oz.
- Cocoa powder – 1 tsp.
- Dark chocolate – 1 tsp.
- Swerve – 8 drops
- Almond butter – 2 oz.

Method

1. Combine all items except the almond butter and then microwave for 30 seconds.

2. Stir and microwave again until everything melts and mixes.
3. Pour the base layer into the mold you are using.
4. Then place a dollop of the almond butter at the center.
5. Fill in the remaining mold on top.
6. Freeze until hard.
7. Serve.

Nutritional Facts Per Serving

- Calories: 297
- Fat: 30g
- Carb: 7g
- Protein: 5g

26. Spiced Cocoa Coolers

| Prep time: 10 minutes | Cook time: 2 minutes | Servings: 10 |

Ingredients

- Heavy whipping cream – 1 cup
- Unsweetened cream – 2 Tbsp.
- Vanilla bean – 1
- Cinnamon – 1 tsp.
- Cayenne pepper – ¼ tsp.
- Erythritol – 2 Tbsp.
- Stevia extract – 20 drops

Method
1. Warm-up cream slightly.
2. Then place all the ingredients in the cream and mix well.
3. Pour the liquid into the ice cube tray and then freeze for 2 hours.
4. Serve.

Nutritional Facts Per Serving

- Calories: 100
- Fat: 5g
- Carb: 1.8g
- Protein: 0.7g

27. Walnut Chocolate and Orange Fat Bombs

| Prep time: 5 minutes | Cook time: 5 minutes | Servings: 8 |

Ingredients

- 85% cocoa, dark chocolate – 4 ½ oz.
- Coconut oil – ¼ cup
- Walnuts – 1 1/3 cups, chopped
- Orange peel – 1 Tbsp.
- Cinnamon - 1 tsp.
- Stevia – 15 drops

Method

1. Melt the chocolate in a double boiler.
2. Mix in the other ingredients.
3. Transfer the mixture into 8 small paper muffins.

4. Refrigerate for 2 hours.
5. Serve.

Nutritional Facts Per Serving

- Calories: 141
- Fat: 8.4g
- Carb: 1.5g
- Protein: 1.5g

28. Coconut Chocolate Candies

| Prep time: 10 minutes | Cook time: 5 minutes | Servings: 9 |

Ingredients

- Coconut oil – 1 cup
- Cocoa powder – 1 cup
- Vanilla bean powder – 1 tsp.
- Powdered erythritol – ¼ cup
- Stevia extract – 15 drops
- Salt to taste
- Coconut butter – ¼ cup, chilled

Method

1. Melt the coconut oil in the microwave.
2. Combine the next four ingredients.

3. Spoon about half of the chocolate mixture into silicone molds.
4. Refrigerate for 15 minutes.
5. Then add ½ tsp. coconut butter into each mold.
6. Top with the remaining chocolate mixture and refrigerate for 40 minutes.
7. Serve.

Nutritional Facts Per Serving

- Calories: 76
- Fat: 7.7g
- Carb: 1g
- Protein: 0.9g

29. Coconut Fat Bombs

| Prep time: 10 minutes | Cook time: 5 minutes | Servings: 12 |

Ingredients

- Shredded coconut – 1 ½ cups, unsweetened
- Coconut oil – ¼ cup
- Butter – ¼ cup
- Cinnamon – ¼ tsp.
- Salt, to taste

Method

1. Preheat the oven to 375F.
2. Toast the coconut on a baking sheet for 5 minutes, then pulse it in a blender.
3. Add the remaining ingredients and stir well.
4. Fill 12 mini muffin cups with 1 ½ tbsp. of the mixture.
5. Refrigerate for 30 minutes.
6. Serve.

Nutritional Facts Per Serving

- Calories: 104
- Fat: 9.6g
- Carb: 0.7g
- Protein: 1.9g

Chapter 3 Savory Fat Bombs

1. Cheesy Jalapeno Fat Bombs

| Prep time: 10 minutes | Cook time: 30 minutes | Servings: 6 |

Ingredients

- Full fat cream cheese – 3 ½ oz.
- Unsalted butter – ¼ cup
- Bacon – 4 slices
- Cheddar cheese – ¼ cup, grated
- Jalapeno peppers – 2, seeded, chopped

Method

1. Preheat the oven to 325F.

2. Line a baking sheet with parchment paper.
3. Lay bacon slices on the parchment.
4. Cook for 30 minutes in the oven.
5. Crumble the bacon into a bowl. Reserve the grease.
6. Blend together the cream cheese and butter. Transfer to a bowl.
7. Add the jalapenos, cheddar cheese, and bacon grease. Mix well.
8. Refrigerate for 1 hour.
9. Make 6 fat bombs out of the mixture.
10. Roll them in the bacon crumbs.
11. Refrigerate for 1 hour.
12. Serve.

Nutritional Facts Per Serving

- Calories: 142
- Fat: 15g
- Carb: 0.7g
- Protein: 3.5g

2. Avocado and Egg Fat Bombs

| Prep time: 10 minutes | Cook time: 10 minutes | Servings: 2 |

Ingredients

- Cooked egg yolks – 3
- Avocado – ½, chopped
- Mayonnaise – ¼ cup
- Lemon juice – 1 Tbsp.
- Spring onions – 2 Tbsp. chopped
- Salt and pepper to taste

Method

1. Boil the eggs for 10 minutes.
2. Halve the eggs. Scoop the egg yolks into a bowl.
3. Blend chopped avocado and the remaining ingredients in a food processor.
4. Mix the avocado mixture with the egg yolks

5. Enjoy with cucumber slices or chopped spring onion on top.

Nutritional Facts Per Serving

- Calories: 147
- Fat: 14.8g
- Carb: 1.1g
- Protein: 2.2g

3. Salmon Bites

Prep time: 10 minutes	Cook time: 0 minutes	Servings: 12

Ingredients

- Smoked salmon trimmings – 2 oz.
- Mascarpone cheese – 1 cup
- Butter – 2/3 cup, softened
- Apple cider vinegar – 1 Tbsp.
- Chopped parsley – 1 Tbsp.
- Salt to taste

Method

1. Smash the cheese with a fork to soften and add the remaining ingredients.
2. Form into small balls, and place on a tray lined with parchment paper.
3. Put in the fridge for 2 hours.
4. Serve.

Nutritional Facts Per Serving

- Calories: 117
- Fat: 13g
- Carb: 1g
- Protein: 3g

4. Salmon Fat Bombs

| Prep time: 10 minutes | Cook time: 0 minutes | Servings: 6 |

Ingredients

- Full fat cream cheese – ½ cup
- Butter – 1/3 cup
- Smoked salmon – 2 oz.
- Fresh lemon juice – 1 Tbsp.
- Dill – 1 to 2 Tbsp. chopped

Method

1. Pulse all the ingredients in a food processor.

2. Line a tray with parchment paper and make fat bombs using about 2 ½ tbsp. of the mixture for each.
3. Refrigerate for 2 hours. Garnish with more dill.
4. Serve.

Nutritional Facts Per Serving

- Calories: 147
- Fat: 15.7g
- Carb: 0.7g
- Protein: 3.2g

5. Bacon and Egg Fat Bombs

| Prep time: 10 minutes | Cook time: 15 minutes | Servings: 6 |

Ingredients

- Hard-boiled eggs – 2, cut into quarters
- Butter – ¼ cup
- Mayonnaise – 2 Tbsp.
- Bacon – 4 large slices
- Salt and pepper to taste

Method

1. Preheat the oven to 375F.
2. Cook the bacon strips on a baking tray for 15 minutes. Reserve the grease.
3. Cut the butter into pieces and add the quartered eggs.

4. Mash with a fork to mix.
5. Add the remaining ingredients except for the bacon and mix.
6. Pour in the bacon grease and mix well.
7. Refrigerate for 20 to 30 minutes.
8. Crumble the bacon.
9. Create 6 balls from egg mixture and roll each ball in the bacon crumbles.
10. Enjoy.

Nutritional Facts Per Serving

- Calories: 185
- Fat: 18.4g
- Carb: 0.2g
- Protein: 5g

6. Bacon and Guacamole Fat Bombs

| Prep time: 10 minutes | Cook time: 15 minutes | Servings: 6 |

Ingredients

- Avocado – ½, peeled, halved
- Butter – ¼ cup
- Garlic – 2 cloves, crushed
- Chili pepper – 1, chopped
- Cilantro – 2 Tbsp. chopped
- Lime juice – 1 Tbsp.
- Onion – ½, diced
- Bacon – 4 slices

- Salt and pepper to taste

Method

1. Preheat the oven to 375F.
2. Cook the bacon strips on a baking tray for 15 minutes. Reserve the grease.
3. Combine the first six ingredients.
4. Season with salt, pepper to taste and mix.
5. Add the onion and the bacon grease and mix.
6. Refrigerate for 20 to 30 minutes.
7. Crumble the bacon.
8. Create 6 balls from the mixture.
9. Roll each ball in the bacon crumbles.
10. Enjoy.

Nutritional Facts Per Serving

- Calories: 156
- Fat: 15.2g
- Carb: 1.4g
- Protein: 3.4g

7. Mediterranean Fat Bombs

| Prep time: 10 minutes | Cook time: 0 minutes | Servings: 5 |

Ingredients

- Full fat cream cheese – ½ cup
- Butter – ¼ cup
- Dried herbs – 2 tsp.
- Sun-dried tomatoes – 4, chopped
- Kalamata olives – 4, chopped
- Garlic – 2 cloves, chopped
- Parmesan cheese – 5 Tbsp. grated
- Salt and pepper to taste

Method

1. Combine butter with the cream cheese.
2. Mash with a fork to mix.
3. Mix in remaining ingredients except for the Parmesan cheese.
4. Refrigerate for 30 minutes.
5. Create 5 balls out of the cheese mixture.
6. Cover each ball with the grated Parmesan cheese.
7. Serve.

Nutritional Facts Per Serving

- Calories: 164
- Fat: 17.1g
- Carb: 1.7g
- Protein: 3.7g

8. Pizza Fat Bombs

| Prep time: 10 minutes | Cook time: 0 minutes | Servings: 6 |

Ingredients

- Cream cheese – 4 oz.
- Pepperoni – 14 slices
- Black olives – 8 pitted
- Sun-dried tomato pesto – 2 Tbsp.
- Chopped fresh basil – 2 Tbsp.
- Salt and pepper to taste

Method

1. Chop pepperoni and olives into small pieces.

2. Combine cream cheese, basil, and tomato pesto.
3. Mix the olives and pepperoni with the cream cheese.
4. Form into balls.
5. Serve.

Nutritional Facts Per Serving

- Calories: 101
- Fat: 9.6g
- Carb: 1.7g
- Protein: 2.3g

9. Cheesy Pesto Fat Bombs

| Prep time: 5 minutes | Cook time: 0 minutes | Servings: 6 |

Ingredients

- Full fat cream cheese – 1 cup
- Basil pesto – 2 Tbsp.
- Parmesan cheese – ½ cup, grated
- Green olives – 10, sliced

Method

1. Mix all the ingredients in a bowl.
2. Serve as a dip with sliced cucumber or other fresh veggies.

Nutritional Facts Per Serving

- Calories: 123
- Fat: 12.9g
- Carb: 1.3g
- Protein: 4.3g

10. Herbed Cheese Fat Bombs

| Prep time: 10 minutes | Cook time: 0 minutes | Servings: 5 |

Ingredients

- Full fat cream cheese – 3 ½ oz.
- Unsalted butter – ¼ cup
- Sun-dried tomatoes – 4 pieces, drained chopped
- Pitted green olives – 4, chopped
- Dried herbs – 2 tsp.
- Garlic – 2 cloves, crushed

- Parmesan cheese – 5 Tbsp. grated
- Salt and pepper to taste

Method

1. Blend together the cream cheese and butter. Transfer to a bowl.
2. Add the next four ingredients.
3. Season with salt and pepper. Mix.
4. Refrigerate for 30 minutes.
5. Make 5 balls out of this mixture.
6. Roll each ball in the Parmesan cheese.
7. Serve.

Nutritional Facts Per Serving

- Calories: 164
- Fat: 17.1g
- Carb: 1.7g
- Protein: 3.7g

11. Pork Belly Fat Bombs

| Prep time: 10 minutes | Cook time: 30 minutes | Servings: 6 |

Ingredients

- Bacon slices – 3, cut in half widthwise
- Pork belly – 5 oz. cooked
- Mayonnaise – ¼ cup
- Dijon mustard – 1 Tbsp.
- Fresh horseradish - 1 Tbsp. grated
- Salt and pepper to taste
- Lettuce – 6 leaves, for serving

Method

1. Preheat the oven to 325F.
2. Cook the bacon slices on a baking sheet for 30 minutes in the oven. Cool.
3. Crumble the bacon into a dish and set aside.
4. Shred the pork belly into a bowl.
5. Mix in the mayonnaise, mustard, and horseradish.
6. Season with salt and pepper.
7. Divide the mixture into 6 mounds.
8. Top with crumbled bacon and serve on top of lettuce leaves.
9. Enjoy.

Nutritional Facts Per Serving

- Calories: 263
- Fat: 26.4g
- Carb: 0.3g
- Protein: 3.5g

12. Stilton and Chive Fat Bombs

| Prep time: 10 minutes | Cook time: 0 minutes | Servings: 6 |

Ingredients

- Full fat cream cheese – ½ cup
- Unsalted butter – ¼ cup
- Stilton – ½ cup, crumbled
- Spring onions – 2, chopped
- Parsley – 1 Tbsp. chopped
- Fresh chives – 1/3 cup, chopped

Method

1. Mix the cream cheese and butter in a food processor.
2. Add the crumbled blue cheese, spring onions, and parsley. Mix well.
3. Refrigerate for 30 minutes.
4. Make 6 balls out of this mixture.

5. Roll each ball in chives.
6. Serve.

Nutritional Facts Per Serving

- Calories: 157
- Fat: 16.2g
- Carb: 0.8g
- Protein: 5g

13. Bacon Ranch Fat Bombs

| Prep time: 10 minutes | Cook time: 15 minutes | Servings: 4 |

Ingredients

- Full fat cream cheese – 8 oz. softened
- Ranch dressing dry mix – 1 Tbsp.
- Bacon – 2 slices

Method

1. Preheat the oven to 375F.
2. Cook the bacon strips on a baking tray for 15 minutes. Cool then crumble.
3. In a bowl, add cream cheese and sprinkle with ranch dressing dry mix.
4. Stir in bacon. Mix well.
5. Form a ball from 1 tbsp. of the mixture.
6. Repeat to form 3 more fat bombs.
7. Refrigerate for 2 hours and serve.

Nutritional Facts Per Serving

- Calories: 419
- Fat: 38.9g
- Carb: 2.7g
- Protein: 11.4g

14. Crispy Savory Bacon Fat Bombs

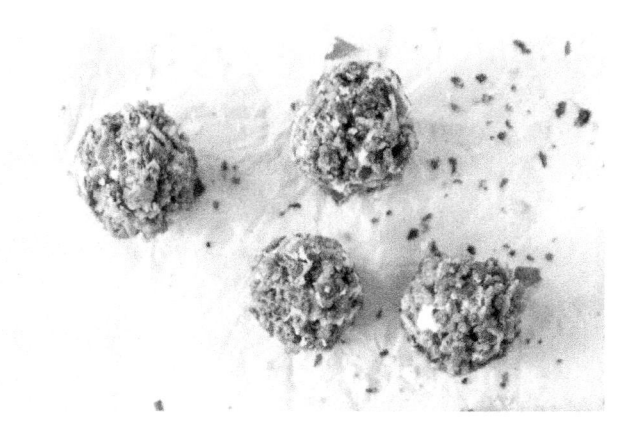

| Prep time: 10 minutes | Cook time: 3 minutes | Servings: 4 |

Ingredients

- Thick bacon slices – 4
- Cream cheese – 4 oz.
- Green chili – 1, seeded, chopped
- Onion powder – 1 tsp.
- Salt and pepper to taste

Method

1. Cook the bacon in a skillet for 3 minutes.
2. Cool and crumble. Reserve the bacon fat.
3. In a bowl, combine the remaining ingredients. Add the bacon fat and mix.
4. Shape the mixture into 4 fat bombs. Refrigerate for 30 minutes.
5. Roll the fat bombs in the crumbled bacon.
6. Serve.

Nutritional Facts Per Serving

- Calories: 141
- Fat: 12.9g
- Carb: 0.5g
- Protein: 5.7g

15. Jalapeno Pepper Fat Bombs

| Prep time: 10 minutes | Cook time: 5 minutes | Servings: 6 |

Ingredients

- Cream cheese – 3 oz.
- Bacon – 3 slices
- Jalapeno pepper – 1, seeded
- Parsley – ½ tsp. dried
- Onion powder – ¼ tsp.
- Garlic powder – ¼ tsp.
- Salt and pepper to taste

Method

1. Fry bacon slices for 5 minutes. Then place on paper towels. Save the bacon grease.
2. Chop the jalapeno pepper. Mix together with bacon fat, cream cheese, and spices.
3. Make balls out of cream cheese mixture and roll them in the crumbled bacon.
4. Serve.

Nutritional Facts Per Serving

- Calories: 101
- Fat: 13.3g
- Carb: 2.1g
- Protein: 4.8g

16. *Waldorf Salad Fat Bombs*

| Prep time: 10 minutes | Cook time: 0 minutes | Servings: 24 |

Ingredients

- Full fat cream cheese – 3 oz.
- Unsalted butter – 2 Tbsp.
- Blue cheese – ½ cup, crumbled
- Green apple – 1/2, peeled, diced
- Garlic powder – ¼ tsp.
- Onion powder – ¼ tsp.
- Chives – 2 Tbsp. chopped
- Pecans – 2/3 cup, chopped

- Salt and pepper to taste

Method

1. Mash together the cream cheese and butter.
2. Add the remaining ingredients except for pecans. Mix well.
3. Refrigerate for 30 minutes.
4. Make balls out of the mixture.
5. Roll the balls in the chopped pecans.
6. Serve.

Nutritional Facts Per Serving

- Calories: 101
- Fat: 19.3g
- Carb: 2.5g
- Protein: 4.5g

17. Brie and Pecan Prosciutto Fat Bombs

| Prep time: 10 minutes | Cook time: 12 minutes | Servings: 1 |

Ingredients

- Prosciutto – 1 slice, about ½ oz.
- Full fat Brie cheese – 1 oz. chopped
- Pecan halves – 6
- Black pepper - 1/8 tsp.

Method
1. Preheat the oven to 350F.
2. Fold the slice of prosciutto in half to make it square.
3. Line a muffin tin with prosciutto.

4. Put the brie on top of the prosciutto.
5. Stick the pecan halves in the middle of the brie.
6. Bake for 12 minutes.
7. Cool and serve.

Nutritional Facts Per Serving

- Calories: 101
- Fat: 16.5g
- Carb: 0.4g
- Protein: 1g

18. Zucchini Fat Bombs

| Prep time: 10 minutes | Cook time: 30 minutes | Servings: 12 |

Ingredients

- Zucchini - 1
- Cream cheese – 3.5 oz.
- Cheddar cheese – 1 oz.
- Unsalted butter – 1 oz.
- Salt to taste

Method

1. Slice zucchini. In a pan, lay slices of zucchini in rows – each with a bit of butter on top and bottom.

2. Add cheddar and cream cheese in the center of each slice, and then sprinkle Parmesan cheese all over. Season with salt.
3. Heat the oven to 220F.
4. Cook for 30 minutes, or until golden.
5. Cool and serve.

Nutritional Facts Per Serving

- Calories: 157
- Fat: 13.6g
- Carb: 0.5g
- Protein: 2g

19. Sardine Fat Bombs

| Prep time: 10 minutes | Cook time: 0 minutes | Servings: 5 |

Ingredients

- Sardines – 3.5 oz. drained
- Unsalted butter – 2 Tbsp.
- Mayonnaise – 2 Tbsp.
- White onion – ½, chopped
- Lemon juice – 1 Tbsp.
- Extra-virgin olive oil – 2 Tbsp.
- Salt and pepper to taste
- Lettuce leaves – 5

Method

1. Mix together the sardines and butter with a fork in a bowl.
2. Add the next five ingredients. Mix again.
3. Season with salt and pepper.
4. Refrigerate 30 minutes.
5. Form balls from the mixture and place on top of the lettuce leaves.
6. Serve.

Nutritional Facts Per Serving

- Calories: 178
- Fat: 17.3g
- Carb: 0.7g
- Protein: 5.1g

20. Smoked mackerel Fat Bombs

| Prep time: 10 minutes | Cook time: 0 minutes | Servings: 6 |

Ingredients

- Full fat cream cheese – 3.5 oz.
- Unsalted butter – ¼ cup
- Mackerel fillet – 1, smoked
- Lime juice – 1 Tbsp.
- Fresh chives – 2 Tbsp. chopped
- Cucumber slices - 6

Method

1. Blend first four ingredients in a food processor.
2. In a bowl, combine the mixture with the chives, and mix with a spoon.
3. Refrigerate for 30 minutes.
4. Serve as a dip with cucumber slices.

Nutritional Facts Per Serving

- Calories: 161
- Fat: 17.3g
- Carb: 0.7g
- Protein: 4.9g

21. Anchovy Fat Bombs

| Prep time: 10 minutes | Cook time: 0 minutes | Servings: 6 |

Ingredients

- Full fat cream cheese – 3 ½ oz.
- Unsalted butter – ¼ cup
- Canned anchovies – 1 oz. drained
- Garlic – 1 clove, crushed
- Parsley – 1 Tbsp. chopped
- Cheddar cheese – ¼ cup, shredded
- Flaked almonds – 1/3 cup
- Cucumber slices – 6

Method

1. Blend first five ingredients in a food processor.
2. In a bowl, combine the mixture with the cheddar cheese and almonds and mix with a spoon.
3. Refrigerate 30 minutes.
4. Serve as a dip with cucumber slices.

Nutritional Facts Per Serving

- Calories: 170
- Fat: 17.2g
- Carb: 1.1g
- Protein: 5.1g

22. Bacon Fat Bombs

| Prep time: 10 minutes | Cook time: 45 minutes | Servings: 6 |

Ingredients

- Bacon – 4 large slices

- Unsalted butter – 1/3 cup, divided

- Chicken livers – 5 ½ oz. diced

- Onion – ½, diced

- Garlic – 2 cloves, chopped

- Fresh sage – 1 Tbsp. chopped

- o   Salt and pepper to taste

Method

1. Preheat the oven to 325F.
2. Cook the bacon slices on a baking sheet for 30 minutes.
3. Crumble the bacon and reserve the bacon grease.
4. In a skillet, heat half of the butter. Add the livers.
5. Cook for 5 minutes. Transfer to a blender and pulse.
6. In another skillet, combine the remaining butter, onion, and garlic.
7. Cook for 10 minutes.
8. Transfer to a blender; add the bacon grease and the remaining ingredients except for the bacon and pulse.
9. Refrigerate for 30 minutes.
10. Make 6 fat bombs from the mixture.
11. Roll them in the crumbled bacon.
12. Serve.

Nutritional Facts Per Serving

- o   Calories: 213
- o   Fat: 19.8g
- o   Carb: 1.2g
- o   Protein: 7g

23. Buttered Bacon Fat Bombs

| Prep time: 10 minutes | Cook time: 30 minutes | Servings: 4 |

Ingredients

- Bacon slices – 4
- Unsalted butter – 4 Tbsp.
- Garlic powder – 1 tsp.
- Pecans – 1/3 cup, toasted, chopped

Method

1. Preheat the oven to 325F.
2. Cook the bacon slices on a baking sheet for 30 minutes. Crumble the bacon.
3. In a bowl, mix remaining ingredients. Refrigerate for 15 minutes.
4. Make 4 fat bombs out of the mixture.
5. Roll each fat bomb in the crumbled bacon.
6. Serve.

Nutritional Facts Per Serving

- Calories: 77
- Fat: 8.1g
- Carb: 0.5g
- Protein: 0.8g

24. Sesame Fat Bombs

| Prep time: 10 minutes | Cook time: 5 minutes | Servings: 4 |

Ingredients

- Butter – 4 oz.
- Sesame oil – 2 Tbsp.
- Sea salt – 1 tsp.
- Chili flakes – ¼ tsp.
- Sesame seeds – 2 tsp. toasted

Method

1. Toast sesame seeds for 5 minutes in a pan. Set aside.
2. In a bowl, mix remaining ingredients.

3. Refrigerate for 15 minutes.
4. Make 4 fat bombs out of this mixture.
5. Roll each fat bomb in the toasted sesame seeds.
6. Serve.

Nutritional Facts Per Serving

- Calories: 123
- Fat: 4.5g
- Carb: 0g
- Protein: 2g

25. Cheese Meatballs

| Prep time: 10 minutes | Cook time: 10 minutes | Servings: 9 |

Ingredients

- Beef – 17 oz. ground
- Mozzarella cheese – 4 oz.
- Parmesan cheese – 3 Tbsp.
- Garlic powder – 1 tsp.
- Olive oil – 3 Tbsp.
- Salt and pepper to taste

Method

1. Cut the cheese into cubes.

2. Combine the dry ingredients with the ground beef.
3. Roll the cubes of cheese with the beef, making 9 balls.
4. Fry the meatballs in olive oil for 10 minutes.
5. Serve.

Nutritional Facts Per Serving

- Calories: 444
- Fat: 28g
- Carb: 2g
- Protein: 46g

26. Scotch Eggs

| Prep time: 10 minutes | Cook time: 20 minutes | Servings: 6 |

Ingredients

- Eggs – 6, boiled
- Pork – 2 oz. ground
- Herbs of choice – 2 tsp.
- Onion flakes – 1 tsp.
- Salt and pepper to taste

Method

1. Hard boil the eggs and remove the shells.
2. Combine the ground meat, the herbs, spices, salt, and pepper.
3. Coat each egg with enough meat mixture to cover.
4. Sprinkle scotch eggs with oil in a lined baking tray.
5. Bake at 350F for 20 minutes or until golden on all sides.
6. Cool, and serve.

Nutritional Facts Per Serving

- Calories: 319
- Fat: 22.5g
- Carb: 0.2g
- Protein: 28.2g

27. Sausage Balls

| Prep time: 10 minutes | Cook time: 20 minutes | Servings: 20 |

Ingredients

- Breakfast sausage - 1 lb.
- Egg – 1
- Almond flour – 1 cup
- Cheddar cheese – 8 oz. grated
- Parmesan cheese – ¼ cup, grated
- Butter – 1 Tbsp.
- Baking powder – 2 tsp.

Method

1. Preheat the oven to 350F.
2. Mix all ingredients in a bowl.
3. Make 20 sausage balls out of the mixture.
4. Put sausage balls on a baking sheet.
5. Bake for 20 minutes.
6. Serve.

Nutritional Facts Per Serving

- Calories: 124
- Fat: 11g
- Carb: 0.2g
- Protein: 6g

28. Mozzarella Fat Bombs

| Prep time: 10 minutes | Cook time: 3 minutes | Servings: 4 |

Ingredients

- Mozzarella sticks – 2, halved
- Olive oil – 2 Tbsp.
- Bacon slices – 4
- Oil for cooking

Method

1. Wrap the mozzarella sticks in the bacon slices.
2. Heat up a pan with oil over medium-high heat.
3. Add the mozzarella stick and cook 1 to 2 minutes per side.
4. Serve.

Nutritional Facts Per Serving

- Calories: 200
- Fat: 15g
- Carb: 4g
- Protein: 4g

29. Cheesy Fat Bombs

| Prep time: 10 minutes | Cook time: 4 minutes | Servings: 4 |

Ingredients

- Mozzarella stick – 12 ounces, cubed
- Sweet paprika – 1 tsp.
- Olive oil – 1 tsp.
- Coriander paste – 1 Tbsp.
- Coconut aminos – 2 Tbsp.
- Ghee – 1 tsp. meted

Method

1. In a bowl, mix the paprika with the olive oil, coriander paste, and the aminos and whisk.
2. Add mozzarella cubes, toss well and leave them aside for 10 minutes.
3. Heat up a pan with the melted ghee over medium heat, add the mozzarella bites.
4. Cook for 1 to 2 minutes on each side.
5. Arrange on a platter and serve with a dip.

Nutritional Facts Per Serving

- Calories: 100
- Fat: 12g
- Carb: 5g
- Protein: 4g

30. Spinach Fat Bombs

| Prep time: 10 minutes | Cook time: 12 minutes | Servings: 30 |

Ingredients

- Ghee – 4 Tbsp. melted
- Eggs – 2
- Coconut flour – 1 cup
- Spinach – 16 ounces, chopped
- Feta cheese – 1/3 cup, crumbled
- Nutmeg – ¼ tsp. ground
- Parmesan – 1/3 cup, grated
- Salt and black pepper to taste

- Onion powder - 1 Tbsp.
- Coconut cream – 3 Tbsp.
- Garlic powder – 1 tsp.

Method

1. In the food processor, mix the spinach with ghee, eggs, flour, feta cheese, parmesan, nutmeg, cream, salt, pepper, onion, and garlic pepper. Blend well and keep in the freezer for 10 minutes.
2. Shape 30 balls out of this mix.
3. Arrange on a lined baking sheet.
4. Bake in the oven at 350F for 12 minutes.
5. Cool and serve.

Nutritional Facts Per Serving

- Calories: 120
- Fat: 15g
- Carb: 4g
- Protein: 4g

CONCLUSION

The Ketogenic diet is comprised of low-carb, moderate protein, and high-fat. Fat Bombs are a healthy combination of high-fat foods, which produce a nutritious explosion of flavor. Often the keto diet can become boring, especially for the beginners. If you are looking for a delicious high fat snack or dessert that help you stay in ketosis, then you need this book. If you are looking for a healthy way to defuse your hunger, fuel your body, and satiate your cravings for something sweet, try these delicious fat bombs!

Printed in Great Britain
by Amazon